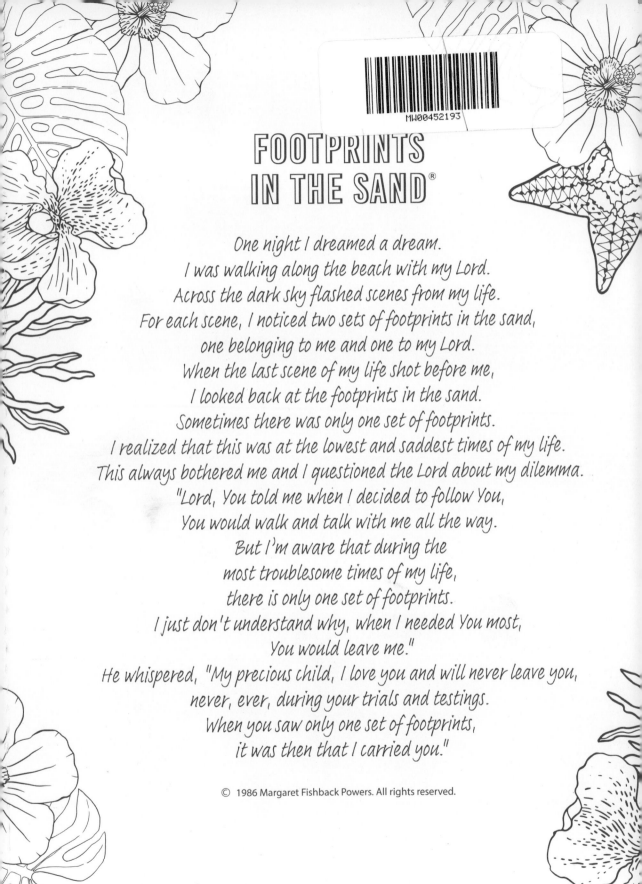

FOOTPRINTS IN THE SAND®

One night I dreamed a dream.
I was walking along the beach with my Lord.
Across the dark sky flashed scenes from my life.
For each scene, I noticed two sets of footprints in the sand,
one belonging to me and one to my Lord.
When the last scene of my life shot before me,
I looked back at the footprints in the sand.
Sometimes there was only one set of footprints.
I realized that this was at the lowest and saddest times of my life.
This always bothered me and I questioned the Lord about my dilemma.
"Lord, You told me when I decided to follow You,
You would walk and talk with me all the way.
But I'm aware that during the
most troublesome times of my life,
there is only one set of footprints.
I just don't understand why, when I needed You most,
You would leave me."
He whispered, "My precious child, I love you and will never leave you,
never, ever, during your trials and testings.
When you saw only one set of footprints,
it was then that I carried you."

This book belongs to _____

Published by Christian Art Publishers
PO Box 1599, Vereeniging, 1930, RSA

© 2023
First edition 2023

Designed by Christian Art Publishers

Cover designed by Christian Art Publishers
Images used under license from Shutterstock.com

Printed in China

ISBN 978-0-638-00039-9

23 24 25 26 27 28 29 30 31 32 – 11 10 9 8 7 6 5 4 3 2

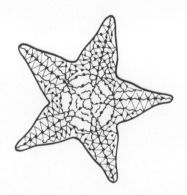

FOOTPRINTS
in the
SAND®

CHRISTIAN ART
PUBLISHERS

One night I dreamed a dream.

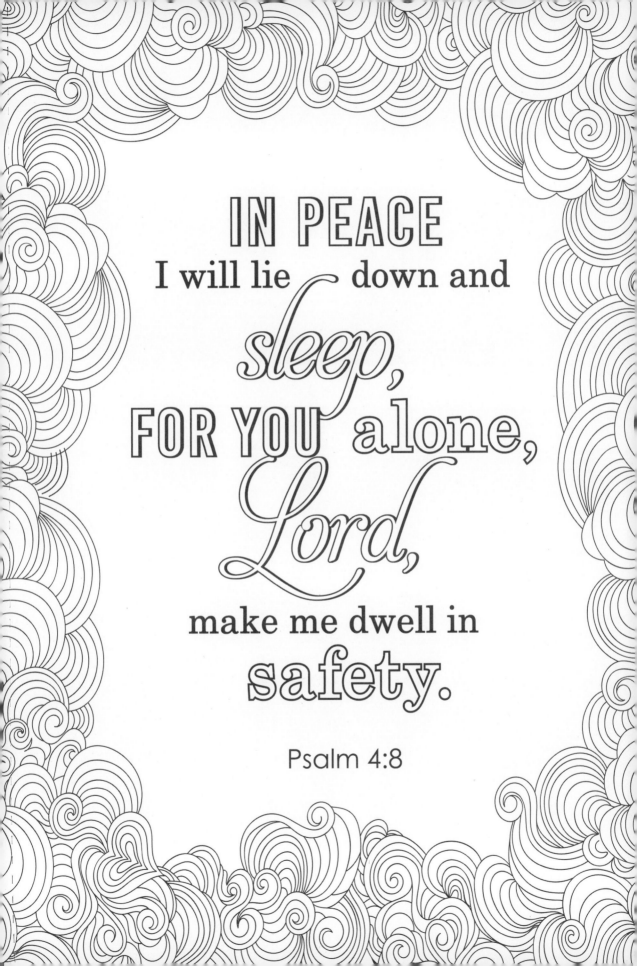

IN PEACE
I will lie down and
sleep,
FOR YOU alone,
Lord,
make me dwell in
safety.

Psalm 4:8

I WAS *walking* ALONG the BEACH with MY LORD.

*I was walking along the beach
with my Lord.*

Across the dark sky flashed scenes from my life.

"I KNOW *the plans* I have FOR YOU."

Jeremiah 29:11

For each
SCENE, I
noticed
TWO SETS OF
footprints
in the
sand.

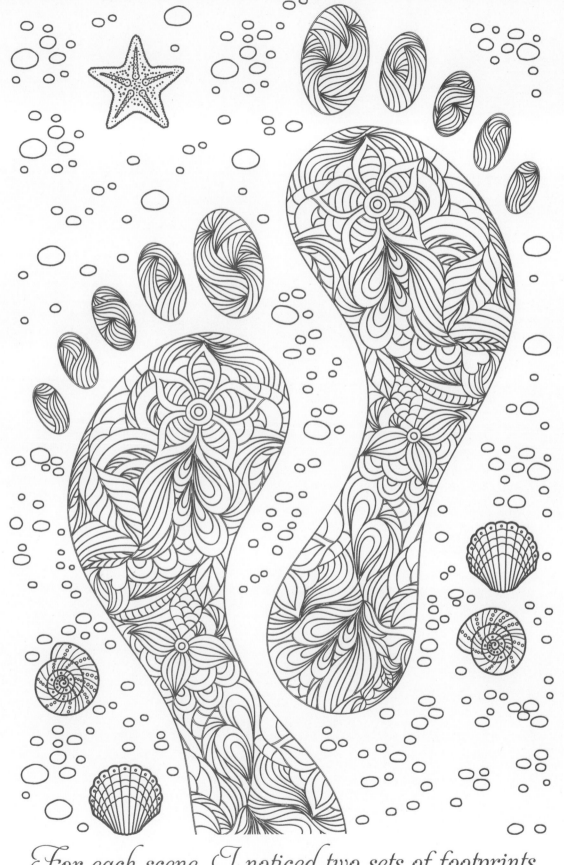

For each scene, I noticed two sets of footprints in the sand.

We
WALK
by
FAITH,
not by
SIGHT.

2 Corinthians 5:7

ONE belonging TO ME and one TO MY LORD.

One belonging to me and one to my Lord.

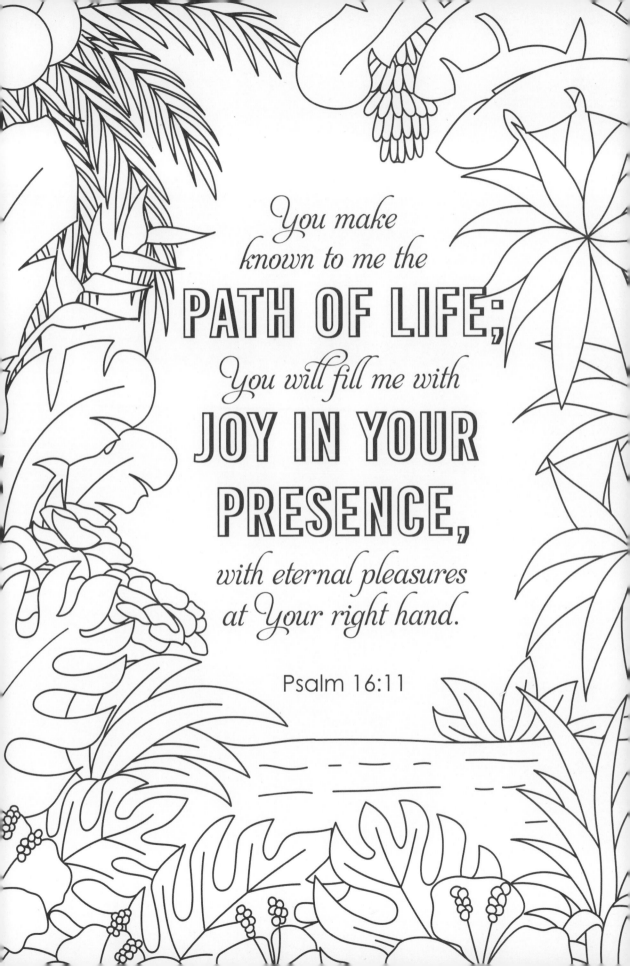

You make known to me the PATH OF LIFE; You will fill me with JOY IN YOUR PRESENCE, with eternal pleasures at Your right hand.

Psalm 16:11

When the last scene OF MY LIFE shot before me, I looked BACK at the footprints IN THE sand.

When the last scene of my life shot before me
I looked back at the footprints in the sand.

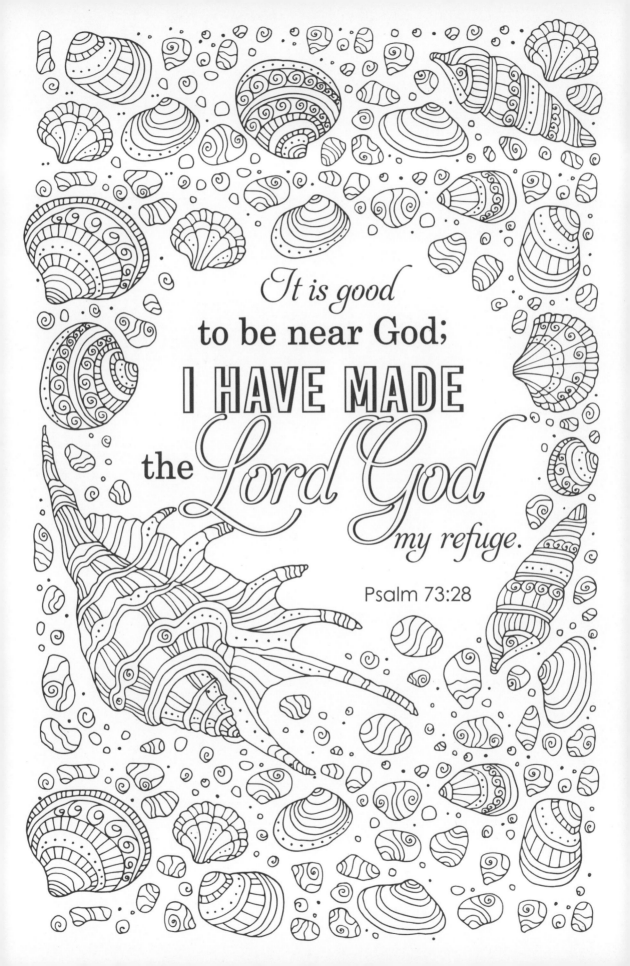

It is good
to be near God;
I HAVE MADE
the *Lord God*
my refuge.

Psalm 73:28

Sometimes there was ONLY ONE set of *footprints.* I realized that this was AT THE LOWEST and saddest times of my life.

Sometimes there was only one set of footprints.
I realized that this was at the lowest and saddest
times of my life.

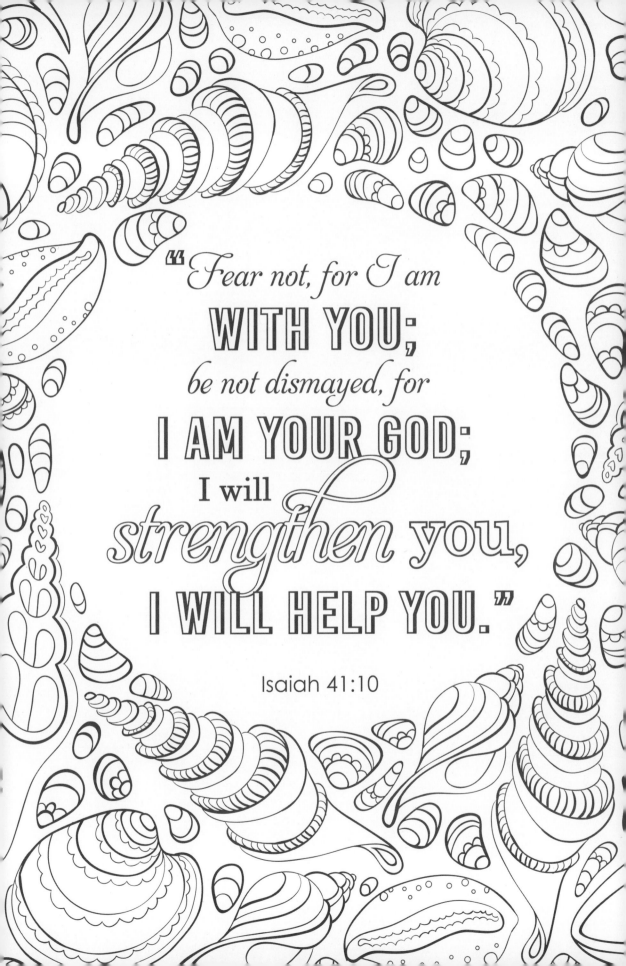

"Fear not, for I am **WITH YOU;** be not dismayed, for **I AM YOUR GOD;** I will *strengthen you,* **I WILL HELP YOU."**

Isaiah 41:10

"**LORD**, You told me when
I decided to *follow You*,
You would
walk and talk
WITH ME all the way.
But I'm aware that during the
most troublesome times
OF MY LIFE, there is only one
set of footprints.
I just don't understand why,
when I needed You most,
YOU WOULD LEAVE ME."

"Lord, I don't understand why, when I needed You most, You would leave me."

Faith is the assurance of things HOPED for, the CONVICTION of things not *seen.*

Hebrews 11:1

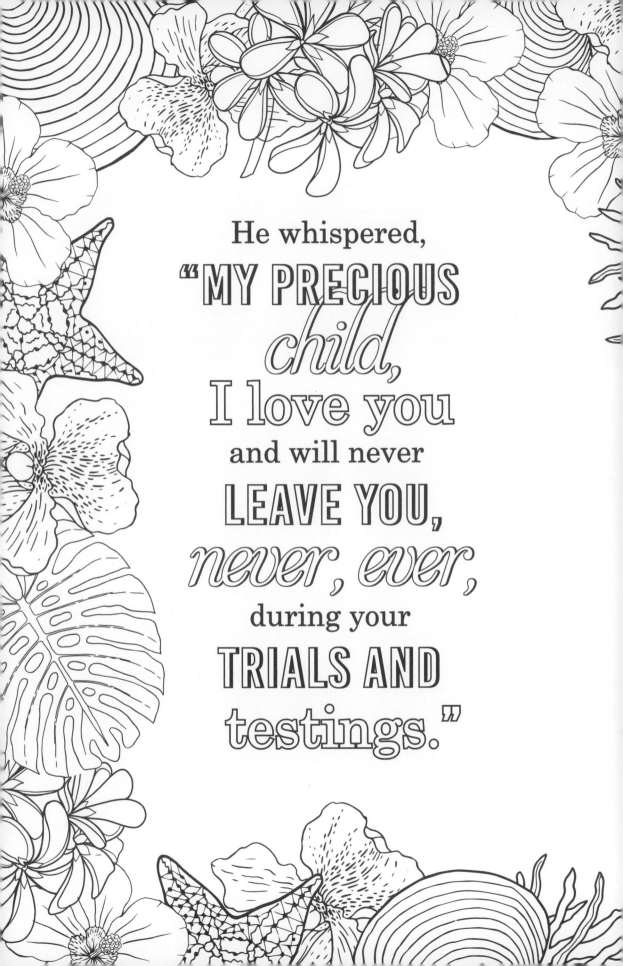

He whispered,
"MY PRECIOUS
child,
I love you
and will never
LEAVE YOU,
never, ever,
during your
TRIALS AND
testings."

He whispered, "My precious child, I love you and will never leave you, never, ever, during your trials and testings."

"WHEN YOU SAW
only one set of
footprints,
it was
THEN THAT I
carried you."

"When you saw only one set of footprints, it was then that I carried you."

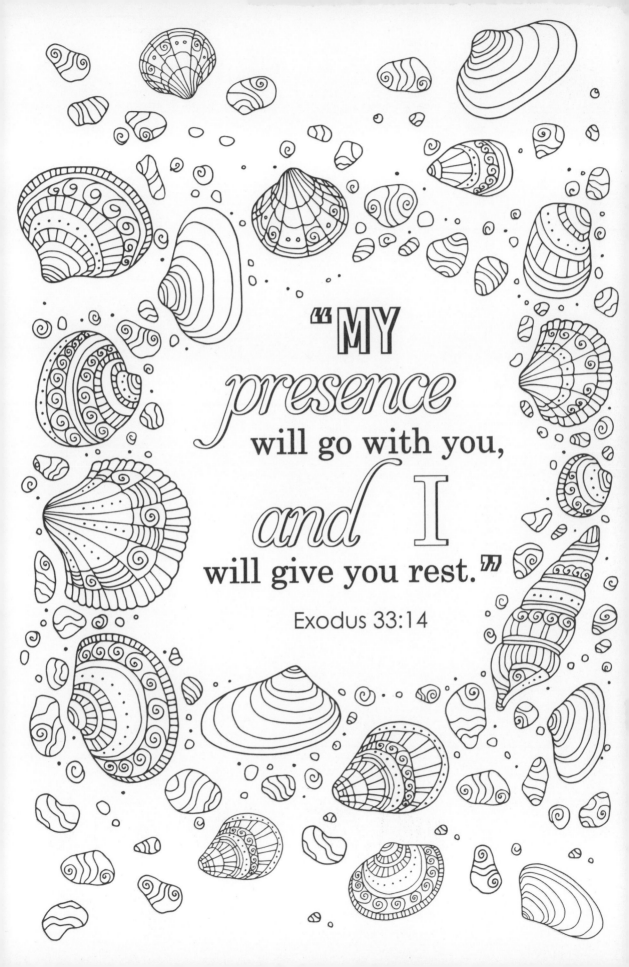

"MY *presence* will go with you, *and* I will give you rest."

Exodus 33:14

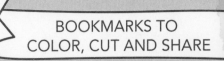

One night I dreamed a dream.

"My precious child, I love you and will never leave you..."

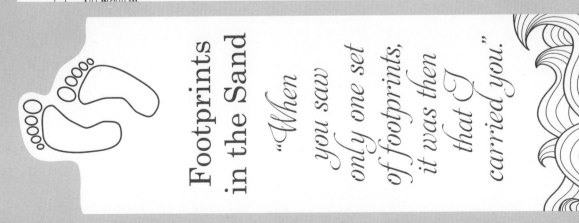

Footprints in the Sand

"When you saw only one set of footprints, it was then that I carried you."

"I am *with* YOU always."

Matthew 28:20

"Don't be AFRAID, *for I am* WITH *you.* *I will* *strengthen* YOU *and* *help you.*"

Isaiah 41:10

We WALK *by* FAITH, *not by* SIGHT.

2 Corinthians 5:7

Leave footprints of *Love & KINDNESS* wherever you go.

TRUST in the LORD with all your HEART and LEAN not on your OWN understanding.

Proverbs 3:5

Dream higher than the sky and deeper than the ocean.

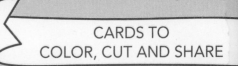

FOLD

FOLD

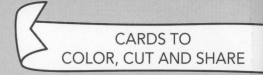

FOLD

Let your
WORRIES
drift away.

FOLD

FOLD

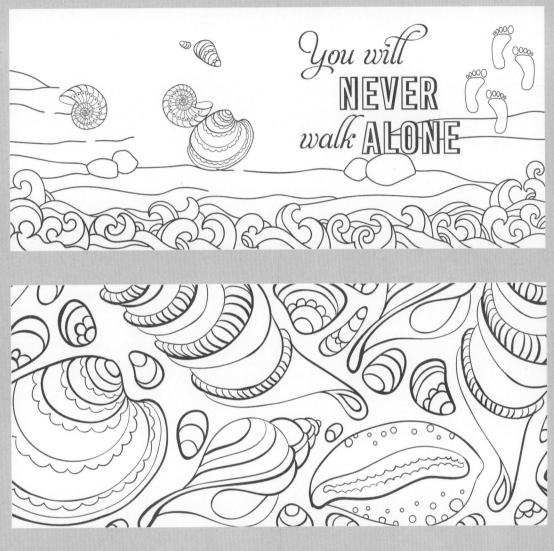

You will NEVER walk ALONE

May God BLESS YOU and KEEP YOU.

FOLD

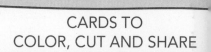

FOLD

FOLD

FOLD

FOLD